Drowning for Shore

Casey Moynihan

Presentation by *BookLeaf Publishing*

Web: www.bookleafpub.com

E-mail: info@bookleafpub.com

ISBN: 9789357441162

First edition 2023

To my son, my greatest love.

ACKNOWLEDGEMENT

Whatever strength I pull from my darkest moments, thank you.

PREFACE

I often think that am I drowning, and no matter how hard and long I swim for, there is no shore. These poems show the real pain in motherhood, and especially single motherhood.

Coaster

For Christmas you made a coaster
of your face, Santa's hat lopsided.
You made a pinched pottery dish
and told me over and over
it can't get wet.
Today I want to fill it with tears
I slam the crayon box
I roll my eyes when you don't eat dinner
I say fuck in front of you
You run and hide and I eat guilt 3 times a day.
A square meal of shame and guilt.
I'll never be the mother you deserve.
We crunch over ice in the field,
waiting for the dog to poop.
You slip and sing,
I hide tears freezing on my cheeks.
Because I can't remember
who I was, or the name of the present you gave
me with your face beaming,
waiting for me to put down the glass.

Five Cardinals

The bus stop has a tree enclosure,
a roof for the dead Hawk we found
on the first day of the year.
Nothing is a bad omen
The Cardinals dart between a yard
and the woods,
peak a boo of red amongst snow covered
branches.
We flip the bird over to inspect its devoured
heart,
brittle rib cage exposed. We don't poke, careful
not to disturb his spirit.
Last spring we found a dead Crow on the other
side of the road, the rainwater moved its body
after every storm.
Closer to the woods, to God, to the wind taking
us home.

Hives

I break out in hives along my jawline
I take deep breaths
I repeat myself 348 times between breakfast and
noon.

The view from our kitchen is a dumpster.
Once a week a truck picks it up
and dumps it out.
People throw away everything-
Here we do not care about reduce reuse, recycle
Here the laundry room has puke in the machine,
spilled dry beans on the floor from a free bag of
food left on the table with solo socks and
dryer sheets. Underwear and soggy cigarette
butts get trapped in between the washer door.
I squeeze the water out all over the floor. I itch
my hives.
This must be my manifestation.

A Rag

We drove an hour to visit friends for an hour.
A new puppy, guaranteed smiles
I noticed your coloring at basketball practice
earlier- ghostly
mot again-
I push thoughts away until they are happening.
By the time the puppy has nipped your ankles,
and the teenagers in the house interrupt my
rambling about a man
my mind wanders to death by whiskey.
I could drown in a bog, peet moss and pain-free.
Your snot rag is soaked
I don't want him snotting all over my blanket-
My normally nurturing mom friend says, and so
we go.
We drive an hour back
Gangsta rap up front- why does it matter, on a
good day I say the F WORD in front of you 3
times.
You sleep, the sight of your ankles wrapped in
tube socks tightens my chest, loosens tears held
in my jaw.

Later I will feel mild anxiety with planning my
40 hour work week

If you're sick, and home, and
Meetings
Treatment plans
Phone calls, cough meds, missed meals, 22
Popsicles, dog walks, missed appointment.
Lugging a feverish kid to the store.

If I call your dad and ask for a Monday visit
instead of a Sunday visit
he will scream, so agitated.

He has to work. Figuring out everything else is
my job.

I know what fire tastes like.

12 MInutes

Into the conversation and you say
defeated
I have to go. Stomach cramps,
migranes, sore bones when it rains.
Bladder infections, UTI, it's been 5 years since
we did something
Just you and I
Pulled shoulder, groin, and neck
Bruises from just walking
what do we expect
Hidden nips, lies are so easy to read coming
from your lips.
Septis, Lyme, fibro, diverticulitis
We can't fight this
I tell you when you say you're sick again, every
3 days
It makes me so helpless I want to shoot myself-
I say that. I think my words are dramatic and
colorful. Just being over the top
 the reason you don't answer, you only have 12
minutes.

Venetian Blinds Give me PTSD

Our son was 3 weeks old-

I flicked them open to moonlight,
burning yellow street light, empty driveway.

Never your car, the one I gave you
braving snow drifts, armed with Tylenol for a
fever
Shoulders for a crutch
Water for a bath

Not even money for gas.
The first winter you had to get snow tires on 4
times.
Not even trying for fresh excuses

I walked on eggshells, cooked you white rice
and fish, swallowed my words dish after dish

You left for 6 days in one time
I lost my mind
I flicked the blinds

The month I met you I dreamt of crows picking
in the bend of my arm, we were on a farm, my
future self was watching
flicking blinds on the dawn.

The house I buy myself will have curtains
Thick and long
the only thing I will walk on is the sound of bird
song.

Chickadee

The song of birds must directly link
to the memory spot in the brain
A sponge of longing
one more summer day then
dusk filled with fireflies
The red picnic table that left splinters
in our palms
Grass blowing
knee high
Raspberries lines the porch.
A light angled for a dirt road

This is where I grew up
I want this for you
The familiar sound of chick a dee dee
dee
We will eat potatoes and apples for a year before
I let this withered apartment be the sound
you remember when you hear a semi on the wet
highway
and call it your childhood memory.

Burnt

We know before we open the box
burnt pizza again. Black pockets
of cheese weighing
down too much sauce
No one wants to point it out
on the couch with a movie
there is too much to be happy about.

Later the bath is filing with shower water. You
love a shower bath.
I remember swimming in my friend's above
ground pool during a rainstorm, so I know why
We used to run in circles to create our own
current, papa don't preach on the radio.
In the bath you are on a search and rescue!
You're a hero, the bath spills water over the edge
Enough to flood the whole bathroom floor. I
decide not to care
You're making your own current
hiding my concern over burnt pizza
and wet floors will rescue us.

Kiss the Cook

The dishes pile
Butterknife standing attention in my orange
mug,
the one I use the most
Something to do with chakras
Something to do with habit
I soak things now like an ex would
Lazy dried yolk
I decided to use my grandmother's plates from
Japan
this way I won't smash them
I yell less when the neighbors are home
I see my own dark spirit splitting all the broken
glass I've ever thrown
What should we eat for dinner
I ask and ask and ask.

Don't want to

I don't want to
Repeat myself
Sit all day
Dream of birds and never play
Kick rocks for fun
Exhaust my soul with no sun
My son
My son
Motherhood is breaking and closing
Opening and sheltering
Missing and being
Lonely and clustered
Shiny and busted.

The worst and best
Hiding in my heart and sewing up my chest
Forget the rest

The Other Boys

The other boys have tablets
but we are here for a party-
I said no
I listen to you beg them to go outside,
you're the only one
It makes me proud enough to burst
but instead I hide with the other moms
Smoke cigarettes on the porch.
By the time you climb into my bed
the next morning
the smell is gone.
You talk about their tablets for days.

Morning

Your tight fist balls on my chest
I open your fingers like an envelope
sticky with sleep
At dreams you cry because you can't keep.
I'm so happy they bring joy.
I still see animals eyes
smoke and running hoofs
Light peering through
a red house in the snow,
I'm left behind, no where to go.
But you, you wake in the morning
wishing to still be there

SOS

In my dream
someone told me I had to say
less
Less words.
Someone.
Fucking.
Help.
Me.

Motherhood is loving so deeply it scares you
one moment
And the next wanting to throw yourself front of
a bus.

Bootstraps

Oh you're a single mom too
It's something, isn't it
this whole do everything everyday by yourself

Oh your mom lives with you
And your grandmother
How nice-
A tribe, I see
So many heads
So many brains to answer
Where flies live
And who made God
And what does a belly look like
split open

Oh your ex gets them every weekend
Every other
Half the week, you say
A real team

Oh you get child support
Like a lot
How smart of you to procreate with old money
Smart girls don't pick between fresh vegetables
and meat

and heat

Oh your ex raised your kids while you went to
grad school
That's cool!
No no
I'm not bitter
That's not what you would taste if you bit me
Try it
Bite me
Have a lick and see how easy your life looks to
me.

Because of you

Daddy visits on Sunday,
and on a good day you don't mention
the planets or how far the sun is.
Because he doesn't know,
and so tells you that no one does.

You have asthma and are allergic
to the dog and dust, and it's like
a damn oak tree is growing in our home. But it's
the jab
And the elite
And the Democrats
And fake science
And this flat Earth seems the reason
Daddy lost all his reason
He shoots lies into his veins now.

Before the pandemic he stored extra food and
worried,
then he mocked the mask
And when he yells at me for everything, why I
ask:
Because of you
Because of you
Because of you.

Fort

I cut a whole in the red blanket
so it can fit over some structure
or another.
You told me your fort was too dark,
but it's from the shadows we made
on purpose.
The way your lips rest during sleep
The way you hum when you eat
From inside your fort our tiny apartment seems
vast
Expanding in proportion to all your questions,
my clever boy.
We can break down any shadows as quickly as
we made them.

Swim

I watch you slip under the surface
and crash back up in a storm of water droplets.
The most natural thing, your feet stretched in the
clear lake water.
Your joy
all my life, I waited for.

First Day

I met you,
I was so confused from the operation,
I don't remember all the details.
You think it's fascinating the way you were cut
from my gut,
the scar peaks just above my bikini bottom.
The darkness of the first night,
in and out of sleep, I tossed
so aware of this little bundle at the end of my
bed.
Even months later when I entered
a room you were sleeping in,
I felt the energy change
Here lies my heart, my cells, my lungs, my life,
my greatest accomplishment and challenge.
Here is my son.